MW00892339

In celebration of

# Guests

# Guests

# Guests

# Guests

# Guests

# Guests

# Guests

# Guests

# Guests

# Guests

# Guests

# Guests

# Guests

# Guests

# Guests

# Guests

# Guests

# Guests

# Guests

# Guests

# Guests

# Guests

# Guests

# Guests

# Guests

# Guests

# Guests

# Guests

# Guests

# Guests

# Guests

# Guests

# Guests

# Guests

# Guests

# Guests

# Guests

# Guests

# Guests

# Guests

# Guests

# Guests

# Guests

# Guests

# Guests

# Guests

# Guests

# Guests

# Guests

# Guests

# Guests

# Guests

# Guests

# Guests

# Guests

# Guests

# Guests

# Guests

# Guests

# Guests

# Guests

# Guests

# Guests

# Guests

# Guests

# Guests

# Guests

# Guests

# Guests

# Guests

# Guests

# Guests

# Guests

# Guests

# Guests

# Guests

# Guests

# Guests

# Guests

# Guests

# Guests

# Guests

# Guests

# Guests

# Guests

# Guests

# Guests

# Guests

# Guests

# Guests

# Guests

# Guests

# Guests

# Guests

# Guests

# Guests

# Guests

# Guests

# Guests

# Guests

# Guests

# Guests

# Guests

# Guests

# Guests

# Guests

# Guests

# Guests

Made in the USA
Coppell, TX
14 April 2022

76565694R00063